Where Should I ?

Ortigia & Syracu

Written by Alex Kerr

Edited by Liberal Publishing House

"Good company on a journey makes the way seem shorter."

Izaak Walton

Thanks for joining me!

Table of Contents

Table of Contents 2

Quick Finder 4

Preface 1

The Journey Begins 1

A Little History 8

Chapter 1 12

Welcome to Ortigia! 12

Chapter 2 18

Tips and Advice on Moving From The U.K. to Europe 18

Chapter 3 29

 A Short Piece on Paradise 29

Chapter 4 34

Fighting and Fear 34

Chapter 5 39

Food, Thoughts and Philosophy 39

Chapter 6 44

Never Turn Down Glaswegians Offering Free Beer 44

Chapter 7 53

Never Bring a Knife to a Mathematician Fight 53

Chapter 8	60
🐱Plays, Performances & Politics🐱	60
Chapter 9	65
🔔 Volcano 🔔	65
Chapter 10	74
A Train Ride to Remember	74
Chapter 11	79
Final	79
Some Helpful Italian Phrases:	81
Being Polite	82
Italian Numbers	83
Directions	84

Quick Finder

Map of Ortigia and Mainland Siracusa	Page 5/6
Map of Ortigia	Page 6
Tips and Advice for Moving Abroad	Page 14
Tomato and pasta Recipe	Page 43
Helpful Italian Phrases	Page 69
Websites to Help With Your Travel	Page 72

Preface

The Journey Begins

The purpose of this book is to keep you company whenever you travel, to keep you entertained if you do or do not while keeping it as close to the truth as possible with the adventures on this sensational island.

This book focuses on Syracuse and Ortigia and aims to show the benefits of living in that town. It is also the first step of a series of books to discuss where is the best place to live in Sicily. There are so many choices that it is almost overwhelming such as Catania, or Palermo, Trapani or Agrigento, or maybe one of the smaller towns or villages scattered over the island.

I lived in London for a second time; in the East End for the first time and enjoyed my time there. I had reignited old friendships and made new ones; I experienced fantastic culture from parks, stadiums, museums, and art in homes, a wide variety of foods from across the globe.

I was recently single and in a job that allows me to be anywhere around the world. The work is for a school teaching online classes of history. I am a history and politics teacher, and this is partly why I am keen on visiting and living on this island. History has been a passion for me since I was at school. As I always attained reasonable grades, it has pushed me further into the depths of our past and Sicily is full of history. I am also a football coach and hold a UEFA B licence. This means I can coach in most parts of the world and in all European football academies. Italy's passion for football is massive and, therefore, another reason I looked at moving out there, although getting a job in football, in a foreign country can be much trickier than you can imagine. There is definitely an element of not what you know, but who you know. I am in my mid-thirties and have always wanted to live by the sea, with the cliché family pressure.

I decided that change was ripe and to sod the family pressure (even if for a few months). I had always had an interest in Sicily and Siracusa, with its history and coast, it seemed like a great first step. Better weather, sea, sun, and sand. With excellent food, a laid-back lifestyle, surfing, snowboarding, culture, cappuccino, calcio (Italian for football), rich history, and the god Vulcan on my doorstep, why had I not done this before? This is one of the many gems on this island and one of the many beautiful islands in the Mediterranean.

To all of you in the U.K. and dealing with the "B" word, I've added this quote, which to me sums up life and which I've posted many times over the years:

'While it's tempting to play it safe, the more we're willing to risk, the more alive we are. In the end, what we regret most are the chances we never took. And I hope that explains, at least a little, this journey on which I am about to embark.'

~ Frasier, Episode: *Good Night Seattle*

On the map below is the island of Sicily. I have highlighted the towns of Catania and Syracuse or Siracusa to give you some context of how to get there. The train system is remarkable in my opinion, considering the volcano, earthquakes, and other issues on the island. It has beautiful, stylish trains with great views of the crystal-clear ocean and Mama Etna on the way to and from Catania and Syracuse or Siracusa (Mama because she is a life bringer to the island.)

This train system works well for Italy and Sicily. Catania is an excellent hub, with a nice airport and easy access to the centre. You can move North to Taormina, South to Noto and Modica, and there are beautiful beaches to the south.

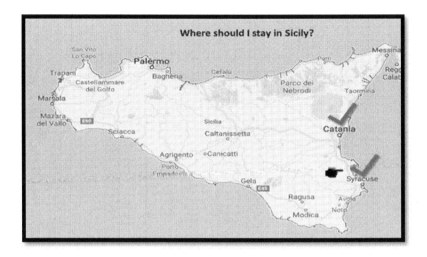

There are nudist beaches for the more adventurous as well, although they tend to be more for the locals and hidden from most tourist books. To the east, you have Palermo, the new capital of the island, which is a few hours away by train, but another beautiful ride through the centre of the island. I've also added a map of Ortigia, which is most likely where you will be spending a good amount of your holiday.

I have not given many names of businesses because part of being a traveller is to find your own experiences but there are enough to give you some idea of where I have been and what I have seen. Below you can see the station, in Siracusa. It's pretty much a straight walk to the island along Corso Umberto.

There are some suggestions for where you can get some great food and drink; all are set in beautiful scenery, but to be fair you're going to find that wherever you go on this island.

On a final note, you might be wondering why I have several spellings for the city. It's because I have found several different spellings for Ortigia and Siracusa. I assume this is in part because of it being occupied by both Greek, Roman and Italian and therefore the spelling has alternated over the years.

On that note, make me a cappuccino. I might be back for breakfast.

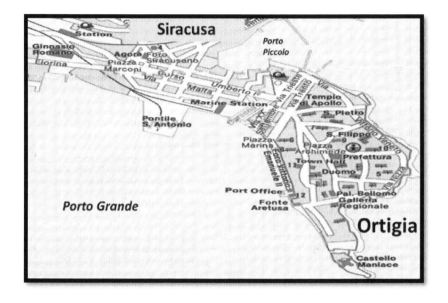

A Little History

***

Syracuse was set up as a city by the Greeks almost 3,000 years ago and has been inhabited ever since, with nearly everyone wanting this island as part of its empire.

The aboriginals, then the Greeks, then the Romans, Normans, Muslims, French, Spanish and finally the Italians were here.

The Greeks landed on the island of Ortigia, (734/733 B.C.) and the city built up quickly, with some of the buildings from the Greek era still existing to this day, including the Duomo, which is based in the main piazza in Ortigia and well worth a visit. It contains the columns and roof from ancient Greece, with stonework from the Normans, and its eventual conversion to the church that it is today.

The city expanded onto the mainland, creating the larger city of Syracuse. Its size and stature rivalled that of Athens, attracting the philosopher Plato to visit and write about his experiences on the island. Eventually, the Roman Empire came knocking and took control of the city in 214 B.C.

It remained mostly under Roman/Byzantium control until 878 AD, when the Muslims began conquering the island. This would sway to-and-fro with the Muslims and Romans until 1085 when the Normans took control of the island. It is said that in the final battle, the fleets clashed in the lagoon next to the city and that the Muslim general fell to the bottom of the lagoon covered in his gold armour.

Fights over the island took place between the Angevin (Eastern European empire) and Aragonese (mainly Spanish-based empire), eventually allowing the Bourbon empire to step in and take charge.

The British became involved in setting up a constitution in 1815, which forced the Bourbon monarchs to flee France during the French Revolution and set up a government in Sicily. To be clear, Sicily is a separate state at this point, and Italy has not been unified as a country since the collapse of ancient Rome. The country has been broken up into smaller states, and some have become exceptionally powerful in history. Venice, Milan, the Papal States and Florence to name a few all had significant impacts on European history over this time.

In 1865, Italy was unified. Ortigia had its walls knocked down and a train station was established on the island, which brings us into the modern period.

Mussolini came to power in 1922 and set about modernising the country into a fascist state with the main street into the island being created. It's now called Corso Giacomo Matteotti, named after a politician who stood up to Mussolini and was kidnapped by Mussolini's henchmen in broad daylight. Interestingly, this almost brought down Mussolini due to the outrage created by the kidnapping.

As you can see, the island has had many suitors fighting for control of this piece of paradise. Hopefully, this book will give you a little insight as to why so many have fought for control of the island. There is also so much more to this history, which I have left out of this book, with the mafia, who still have power and influence, or the Phoenicians, who also established colonies on the island.

Chapter 1

Welcome to Ortigia!

***

Welcome to Ortigia, the island of Plato, Archimedes and Caravaggio.

My first week on the island and I feel as if I've settled into life quite quickly. With a beach and sea lifestyle and a smattering of Italian, it's easy to see how.

My arrival by plane to Catania was simple enough; the airport was fine and modern, with styled marble flooring. English and Italian language everywhere. Catania is a sizeable, beautiful town north of Syracuse. Getting to Syracuse provided more unexpected difficulties. In my naivety and positive thinking, I expected transport to be frequent and easy for this popular, beautiful and once rival to Athens city. However, it was spring when I arrived so there was a limited amount of public transport.

After 6 pm, there were only three more buses and no trains, so I sat and waited for three hours for a bus. Thankfully, due to the diligence and standards set by all Italians, there was decent quality food in the airport, and with the exchange rate and living standards, it was cheap. So, I sat eating an aranchia: a medium-sized, egg-shaped dish made of a tomato-based sauce, mixed with mozzarella and rice. The bus arrived. People were helpful. I sat at the back of a non-air-conditioned bus for an hour and a half. Due to a lack of air-conditioning, the bus quickly became so hot that I didn't take in the views and I quickly passed out. I awoke to a "Thank you."

I think my Italian was still rusty at this point, and the brain groggy. I found a young Italian man next to me, also passed out and his friends behind, leaning in to take photos of both of us, I believe with eyes closed and mouths wide open they had taken delight in the scene. I did not know the Italian for "sod off."

I'll be adding that to my list.

Upon arrival, I was picked up by my host and taken to my apartment via a Vespa moped, a classic start to an Italian adventure. The brilliant resilience of the host didn't stop my giant luggage bag being stowed onto the back with rope, cables and some Sellotape! As we drove to the island city, the buildings became more ancient and romantic, with an intense colour of sandstone soaking up the spring sunshine. We circled through the buildings and streets until we got to the closest parking point, and then it dawned on me how old the city was. Words paint a picture, but there is nothing like venturing into the painting.

The city is divided into two parts the mainland and the island, which causes rivalry with locals. There is the mainland, known as Syracuse, and there is the island, which is where the first settlements were started, called Ortigia. This was where I was headed.

As we closed in on the island, two bridges connected the mainland to the island. We crossed the narrow streets, some filled with plants climbing the ancient sand-coloured crumbling walls, palm trees and ivy, and flowers draping down from the balconies and the smell of fresh salty air. The balconies were thin and rustic, with intricately patterned buttresses that hold up the platform and overhang onto the street. I'm yet to see a free runner abuse these narrow streets or a scene from *Romeo and Juliet* take place upon the balconies.

The first thing I noticed was that under a lot of the balconies there was green netting. This is to keep the concrete underneath from falling on passers-by. There was, however, nothing to stop the concrete falling through the green netting and some were filled to the brim. Comical scenes played through my head of Romeo wearing a hard hat or being knocked unconscious.

As it was early afternoon, the sun shone through the streets and gave off a warm glow. As I walked, I felt I was in a lovely residential area, but quickly realised it was more than that. As I looked left and right, I could see family shops selling food, clothing and puppets.

The puppet theatre, it turns out, is a historical speciality for Syracuse and, I believe, Sicily. I'm yet to see a show.

Finally, arriving at the flat, I found there were two pizzerias just next to and directly under my balcony. Perfect.

The apartment was booked through Airbnb and seemed just as rustic as the streets. A rusty steel gate, twice my width, a double wooden door, and then up some stairs to the front door. It was simply designed, tall in height, with a kitchen, bedroom and a bathroom, but inside the bathroom was a spiral staircase, leading to a terrace, complete with table, chairs and garden canopy. *Welcome to Italy,* I thought, as I settled and unpacked into my new home.

If you would like to know more information on the buses, I am happy to suggest you use: Checkmybus.

https://www.checkmybus.co.uk/catania/siracusa

Chapter 2

Tips and Advice on Moving From The U.K. to Europe

***

Before you leave:

I've been using the website MSE, money-saving expert, and it's packed full of decent and entirely up-to-date advice. If you're looking for insurance for travelling, moving abroad and sports, there is a page on the site that helps you find cheap insurance.

https://www.moneysavingexpert.com/travel-insurance/

This has become particularly useful as I broke my tooth on a wasabi pea as I sat on the plane for a second visit in September. Dental and medical reasons for a return to the U.K. were covered! After seeing the bill presented to me from the Sicilian dentist for a root canal, I could not help but feel I had been saved from two painful experiences. As the site states, the medical costs can be quite expensive. However, you can have some coverage for as little as £9 for the year.

I would read the small print. I once lost my bags on an internal flight in the US and, because it was internal, I wasn't covered. This can apply to missed domestic flights as well as the return flight.

Getting There:

For booking flights, I would recommend Sky Scanner. It's pretty simple to use, website or app.

https://www.skyscanner.net

The site has saved me hundreds, if not thousands, of pounds over the years. It even has a few cool features such as a global map that can help you choose locations and it has all the prices from your destination to lots of sites across Europe.

E.U. Trainline:

This is another brilliant resource for getting around Europe.

https://www.thetrainline.com/trains/europe

I've found trains that take you from Sicily to Genoa to Marseille (if booked far enough in advance) for €25. It might take longer, but it can be a beautiful train ride and much cheaper than the airlines during peak travel times. More on this later, with a fantastic journey from Syracuse to Rome.

Spending Money:

Metro Bank

https://www.metrobankonline.co.uk/

At present, getting this card costs nothing. Just open an account, in-branch (mainly based in London), and that's it: You can use their card for no fee. On top of that, if you open a second account, you may request a spare emergency card at no extra cost.

Getting the lingo:

Duolingo:

This app is entirely free and will teach you languages. Even some basics such as thank you, yes, no, and please, really can go a long way to helping you establish yourself in another country. Consider doing this for 5 minutes a day the month before you go out. This friendly learning device is easy and quick to use and has helped me on many occasions.

However, for those wanting to learn, the Oxford language books and listening guides have been phenomenal. The one I am currently using is called *Take Off In Italian, 2004.* Download it to your PC via iTunes, then listen to it at your convenience. If you're travelling on public transport and can get the book out, I can't recommend it enough. Chapters are based on scenarios, such as cafes, or restaurants, or meeting the family. Even a little dating. *"When in Italia"*.

If you've got the cash and some time, see if you can find a local language school. They are usually a little pricey but if you add in the above, it should have a multiplying effect. Plus, it's nice to know there is someone you could go to and ask for advice or help with the culture and who speaks your language. My experience so far has been great, my Italian has picked up quickly, and I've been able to learn about different parts of the culture. Last week, I requested a lesson on haggling in the market. It was fun, funny and entertaining to role play and well worth it. Plus, we went down to the market together for a lesson in both.

Finally, if worse comes to worst, download Google Translate. It's free, you can talk into it, and it will automatically translate for you.

Talking and Some Other Advantages:

Three Mobile

www.three.co.uk

They have a fantastic offer. They will give you access to other phone companies in Europe and large parts of the world for free for two months. It also provides you with your minutes and 16GB of internet usage. However, after those two months, you might be cut off as this is only meant for travellers; not moving abroad. Two months should be enough to get yourself established, and have enough of the language to go to a local phone store.

Living, Adventure and Romance:

Airbnb, housing/experiences:

Some of my most fulfilling and amazing experiences have been through Airbnb. I've gained jobs, girlfriends and friends for life as a result of this company. A few September's ago, in New York, I stayed in a hotel near Central Park. I was enjoying my time in the city. It was sunny with a cool autumn breeze. The trees were changing colour. It was a lush brown and orange set of colours as I jogged through Central Park every morning over bridges and through piles of crisp and crunching leaves. I loved every moment, buying coffee and books, and reading Jack Kerouac.

However, I realised that I was not getting into the culture. I met people from the hotel, but there weren't many Americans and no New Yorkers. It then dawned on me that I could be anywhere in the world and that the hotel gave me little connection to the city and its culture. I decided to try Airbnb and see if I could get a different taste of life and possibly embed myself in the culture a little more.

One of my first efforts was to stay in Brazil; my offer on Airbnb was to stay with anyone who could get me access to a football club. I couldn't believe it when I ended up having entry into two of the most prominent clubs in Brazil and later gaining work experience and friends from the club. I also made a friend for life. A caring, lovely lady, who had travelled the world as a journalist and had lived in the EU and spoke near-fluent English. We got on like a house on fire, and still talk to this day. Her review of me was one of the most unexpected and beautiful pieces of writing I'd ever had about me. Not only that, I moved to another part of Brazil, the island of Santos, and decided to do it again. I organised a stay in another shared flat. I ended up meeting a future girlfriend. She arranged to pick me up from the football club. I was stunned by her looks. I even thought, *"I don't stand a chance with this lady."* She admitted that there was a possibility I would not be able to stay at her family house, as her aunt was visiting the family. By the end of the evening, I had been invited to a Brazilian birthday and had then been taken out to meet the lady's friends on a tropical Brazilian beach. By the end of the evening, in a fresh soft breeze, she was in my arms, kissing me as ocean waves lapped against our ankles. Do, or can, hotels offer experiences like this?

This is just one of my many adventures with Airbnb and I'll possibly write about that in a future book.

Keeping Fit and Meeting People:
Gym

I picked a location with beaches and warm waters. So, working out in the morning at home, then getting down to the beach early morning, then swimming, became my new life regime. However, going to the gym has always been in my routine, but I've also felt it has been a plus when moving abroad. It gets you into a particular part of the culture. It keeps you active; you get to at least see, if not meet, people. It gives you a different activity if you are struggling to find a life routine when you first arrive.

There was an excellent gym near the centre, but the owner went to follow his dream in Germany of being a bodybuilding champion. The next gym is over the bridge, onto the mainland. Then it is almost a straight line. You need to go past the Santuario della Madonna delle Lacrime Palazzetto Church, (You can't miss this church it is the biggest building in Siracusa.) past the park the Parco Giovanni Paolo II where you will come to Concetto Lo Bello. I've not been inside, so I can't fully recommend but if you are keen, please check it out and let us know on the blog.

https://welcomeworldwalker.com/

Meeting Locals:

My final thought and observation is to find a few spots you like and keep going there. You will eventually get to know the staff and you'll feel more settled. It's amazing how much a friendly face or a warm smile can make a difference when moving abroad on your own, even though you've no idea what they are saying.

I've also found the importance of names to be very significant. You might have to learn the phrase, *"What's your name?"* but it makes such a difference when you've met them a second time, you've remembered their name and, hopefully, they've remembered yours.

"Remember that a person's name is to that person the sweetest and most important sound in any language"

~Dale Carnegie.

Chapter 3

A Short Piece on Paradise

***

Back to the adventure. It is a paradise. I sit here, writing this in 20C weather, the May sun gently gliding to the hills over the blue lagoon, sipping on cocktails, listening to soft Brazilian bossa nova, all costing little to nothing. Yep, "git" is right, if that's what you are thinking.

The lifestyle here is so juxtaposed to London. The city of London has so many things attached to it, and inside it, that helps to make London genuinely fabulous for its own reasons. Dr Johnson was right when he said, and I paraphrase, "When you are bored of London, you are bored of life."

However, there is an alternative to life in London. London can offer so many activities and new places to visit, mixed with great food, history and culture that is hard to beat. Yet out here, on the island of Ortigia, which is and is not connected to the city of Syracuse, there is a special sense of paradise. If you are bored here, you can be bored with life too. On the day of writing this, I have reached one month in the city, and I feel I have settled, but I've obviously only been here over a short space of time. The island of Ortigia is a labyrinth of streets that wind and curve throughout the island. The island is connected to the mainland by two bridges. You never genuinely feel lost or worried about crime. The island does have streets for cars but it is mainly pedestrianised; the streets for cars are few and far between, yet cars are still able to drive their way through the centre of the city, through what seem like impossible angles to drive through or corners that defy logic. They beep their horns to get you to move when behind you, causing you to suppress your annoyance and wanting to punch the bonnet for the fact they've disrupted your tranquil walk. #Hulk. I do make a joke on this point, but because it is so peaceful, the sound of a horn stands out far more than in a big city. The rest of the time it is as peaceful as a newborn lamb, on a sunny spring day, hooked on morphine.

The weather feels like a constant spring. Temperatures never get below 17C and never above 24C since I've been here, causing you to want to go out and catch the rays every day. This seems to add a lovely and calm touch to people's personalities (except when driving).

You will see people just happy to walk along the seafronts, day in and day out. Smiles beaming across their faces in the sun, with ice cream or cannoli in hand (Cannoli is an excellent Italian dessert, which will be talked about later.) This brings me nicely onto the food. I've foreign-to-the-U.K. girlfriends and British friends ask me, 'Why do you put spices on your food?' In my opinion, I've found certain vegetables in Britain lacking in flavour, and they've needed something extra to enhance it. Not here; I've cooked quite a bit in Sicily, and I've not added salt or pepper once. All the tomatoes, basil, celery and fruit have been perfect on their own. A splash of olive oil and you are done. Whilst eating out is cheap and tasty as well there is almost always a shop and a restaurant serving some of the most delicious and delightful food you can imagine.

Surprisingly, it's generally cheaper to head to the restaurant for some pizzas than to ever buy from the market. To this point, it has inspired me to hit the local outdoor markets and grab fish and squid and find equally simplistic recipes to cook and experiment with. I even helped some Canadian tourists, who seemed lost in the city centre. They asked my advice for some decent restaurants, and as soon as they told me they were staying in an Airbnb, with kitchen facilities, I immediately suggested that they go have fun in the market and cook a meal. I was immediately invited to join the family and friends for a meal that night! I picked up some great wine, and the food they put on was incredible; they had scoured the markets and one of the hosts happened to be an excellent chef. Spaghetti in ragu, with hors-d'oeuvres/tapas dishes galore, all fresh; artichokes, sun-dried tomatoes, bacon covered asparagus, fresh fish and salads. Wine and spritz flowed all night long with other random locals who had also been invited after meeting these lovely Canadians.

Chapter 4

Fighting and Fear

***

Warning: Paracetamol & sun cream does not stop lava.

This evening, I'm writing at a nice spot in front of a fountain.

I've been tempted by the idea of writing about facing fears. I have been working on several books and one is on warfare. Being here and working on it, the day was set aside as a public holiday in Italy to commemorate its independence from fascism. It reminded me of my great uncle who had told me how during World War Two he had landed in Sicily and had landed in Normandy on D-Day. So, during some research, I discovered that they either landed in Syracuse or just south of here. Strange to think the last family member to be here was possibly fighting in these very streets. Talk about facing your fears. Yet, when you listen to that generation, and how they faced it, you will often hear statements like: 'It was what we had to do,' or 'I didn't want to be away because that meant someone else had to pick up the slack I had created."

Earlier, I had quoted from a show about a psychologist who had decided he needed a new adventure.

"While it's tempting to play it safe, the more we're willing to risk, the more alive we are. In the end, what we regret most are the chances we never took."

~Frasier, *Good Night Seattle* episode.

Instead of staying, he left and moved to a new city. It seemed to me that the point was to face a fear of the new and unknown, to go on an adventure regardless of age, a final hurrah that you hear from writers such as Bill Bryson, or the adventures of Baron Von Munchausen. I can't compare fighting in the streets to moving to a new town and country. Yet it was interesting to hear from my gran recently that she thought I had been brave in just moving, being alone, not speaking the language, just doing it and going, and this lady had lived through bombings during World War Two. An interesting thought, and not something I would agree with.

Naturally, bravery comes in many forms, and it's been interesting so far, being here in a city that's in constant danger, with Europe's most active volcano on its doorstep, which according to new data, is slowly slipping into the sea. I've been here for approximately 6 weeks, and I have already taken more steps to be protected from volcanos and earthquakes than I ever did during all the time I lived in London or the U.K., bearing in mind the many terrorist threats that exist in the capital.

Earthquakes seem to hit Italy every 2 – 3 years, and Mount Etna appears to be irregular but still active. I read a story from 1669, where villagers from Catania went up to the volcano and bravely fought off the volcano's lava flow, which was headed towards the village. They took wet sheepskins, pickaxes and shovels, and saw some success in changing the direction. However, they were chased off the mountain by people from Paterno, a neighbouring town, who felt that the lava flow was being pointed in their direction! Despite their efforts, the lava still made its way to Catania.

So, based on these stories and events, I actually have a prepared bag, with everything from a Swiss Army knife to sunscreen and paracetamol.

I think one of the nicest things I've heard since I arrived here is actually from a friend, who took on a small fear. Every morning this week I have headed to the beach first thing in the morning, to sit in the glorious sunshine on a hot beach, then to jump into a mildly warm sea and swim out to the seaweed. A friend mentioned she had never snorkelled and had a slight fear of it so she and her friend decided that morning to just go and try it out. After 20 minutes, I jumped in and swam out to join them. As I joined, I asked, "How was it?"

She said, "Fine, I enjoyed it."

Foolishly, I then mentioned how I had not swum this far out before and that it was deep. I then pointed out I sometimes had to resist playing that *Jaws* music. Suffice to say, we quickly came ashore.

Three weeks after I left the island, Mount Etna did erupt, forcing the surrounding air space to be closed as a layer of ash blanketed parts of the island. Two days later an earthquake of a magnitude of 4.8 on the Richter scale shook the town of Catania. The flight I took to return to the U.K. flew over the top of the volcano and through its ash cloud!

Chapter 5

Food, Thoughts and Philosophy

***

I found this car in the streets of Ortigia full of oranges. I've never really seen anything quite like it before.

A gem of thought was uncovered to me. In the last chapter, I discussed some ideas of bravery or courage. I had signed up for some university-style seminars on Plato and philosophy, which were to be hosted on the island of Ortigia, an island he had visited on 2 or 3 occasions.

I had a week to prepare, and the cocky me reared up and felt I could get through a large chunk of Plato's material in a week. In preparation, I started reading books on Plato and reading his works with an app called Scribd.

One of the first topics that I read from Plato's dialogues was courage and how to define the word.

"The ability to do something that frightens one; bravery."

~Oxford Dictionaries definition

In this account, Plato writes a play mainly written in dialogue (thus, the name of the books *The Dialogues*) where he places his mentor, Socrates, in discussion with others from Athena, on what is courage or bravery. The premises are many; Socrates is aware that he has no way to truly define the word courage or bravery but is aware that people do think in their minds they can define the word. Socrates won't allow this and, through asking questions, begins to dissect the definitions.

Bravery is an incredible piece to discuss: One I had not had much thought of attempting to define but have always felt is evident in its meaning and universally understood. You can be brought to many conclusions or no conclusion, as bravery is a blurred line. When you think you are close to defining it, it slips through your hands and fingers like sand or water. It can be brave or reckless; it can involve luck, fearlessness or doing something that is wise or good, and hopefully both. This then leads to another discussion of what is wise and what is good, which I will leave for another talk.

Suffice to say it was an interesting debate to have and one you could have with yourself.

The seminars themselves were extraordinarily fruitful and thought-provoking. There were professors from all over the world, all there to debate Socrates and Plato's views and works, with a heavy emphasis on the definition of beauty. The Greeks even had a distinct set of parameters. One included on the body was the second toe being longer than the big toe, which was very beautiful.

The week flew by, with discussion and debate with many colleagues over numerous issues that arose from the week-long seminar. It was based on the professors' reading pieces they had prepared on various topics relating to love and beauty, then questions and answers at the end, sometimes extending into discussions and debates with everyone there. Lunch and dinners were provided; unlimited coffee and cake were eagerly eaten. The evenings were filled with culture, from tours of the museums, the archaeological park and tours of the city. The final night was wrapped up in a boat ride around sunset and a slap-up meal.

The meal was quite amazing, traditional Sicilian dishes of fresh fish, shrimp and squid. Courses of pizza and pasta with unlimited wine, mixed with Sicilian song and dance.

Even I was put to shame by the never-ending supply of food. I had to quit on the 8/9th course! Sumptuous and delicious delicacies from the sea, piled onto our table. Squid, zuppatta, pasta dishes, anchovies in lemon, fried fish and I swear there was pizza as well. This was all blended in with conversations of Plato, politics, Spartans, Socrates, the mafia and Mussolini, with copious amounts of wine. The evening flowed, and I even came away with potentially co-authoring a book, a few more friends scattered across the globe and some food for thought.

If you would like to attend the seminars that take place in Siracusa. I have attached a link below to their site:

http://www.fontearetusa.org

Chapter 6

Never Turn Down Glaswegians Offering Free Beer

***

The sun sets; orange and blue colours mix in the water as I sit pondering what am I to write about this week, when two Glaswegians sit down next to me, eating ice cream, and the conversation begins to flow on Sicilian food and they eventually offer to buy me a beer to allow the conversation on Sicilian food to continue.

My week has been one of culture. I'm not debating the meaning of this word or any other in this chapter. The island is just full of it; in language, food and history. From the Odyssey landing on the island and taking out its cyclops to the sirens north of here singing beautiful music to lure sailors into the rocks. However, I thought I'd focus on my experience with food culture.

The cuisine is a mixture of Greek, Latin, Arabic and Spanish. There is clearly an Italian base for the cooking. Locals tell me that the food that is grown on the island does not need fertiliser or pesticides due to the nitrogen and other materials spread by the volcano. There is also the sea, which is another source of the food here, and Mount Etna, it could be argued, is another source. The nickname for Mount Etna is Mama Etna; Life-giver, provider and potentially scary as hell. Read into that what you may.

The volcano contributes to the quality of the food, as it spreads nitrogen-rich ash over the island. Add some water to quench the thirst of plants and you have a bonanza food supply.

A reflection on my experience with some female Sicilian friends who have experienced my cooking and have trusted me as far as they could throw me (apparently their experience with Englishmen in the kitchen has been somewhat dire) is that when

I've cooked for them, I've had to tap them with a wooden spoon and give them glaring looks to remove them or stop them interfering with the cooking process.

Food is of paramount importance. There are cooking styles and essential rules. You don't mess with tradition and I've have had arguments with Sicilians over how to cook certain dishes and over what ingredients can be added. You might argue as to what do I know? I've run a restaurant for a start, and I've been cooking large amounts of Italian food for quite some time, lasagne being a personal favourite of mine, as well as risotto, pasta, basil pesto and gnocchi, also following recipes to the letter from famous chefs to experiment with. The final compliment and certificate of authenticity have come from the Sicilians themselves who have eaten healthy portions of my food with wide smiles and happy eyes; I think the highest compliment I could have possibly received. Even though they initially rejected my selection of ingredients, they soon guzzled it down upon the first taste.

One of my favourite dishes is from the sea. The seafood here has been fantastic; cozze (mussels) has been a favourite, which I cook in lemon, celery (an ingredient of many arguments), white wine, garlic and water. It takes 7 minutes to cook and comes out with a beautiful sweet flavour. Here is the best bit: While this has been cooking, I've also been preparing a main dish of pasta and a salsa sauce (tomato base), tomatoes fried in olive oil and a single anchovy, until soft, then adding celery, garlic and passata with some basil. I take the water from the mussels and pour it over the pasta, leaving it to soak in the ocean flavours. Once this has almost entirely cooked, I add the pasta to some heat until cooked, leaving the salsa on low heat or off, all the while eating and nibbling on the mussels. I then normally mix the salsa and cooked pasta and cook for one minute to blend the flavours. One thing you will note is that with these recipes, I've not added any salt or pepper. In fact, since I've been here, I've not added any spices at all. The food is just that tasty on its own. Mama Etna provides the flavours.

There is also squid, although be careful as removing their guts can be difficult and will resemble a scene from *Alien*. Their ink sac can be a threat, and for that reason, glasses/goggles should be worn. They tend to spray, potentially making beautiful modern art, which is a pain to clean afterwards. There are many other dishes to talk about, which I'll save for another book or maybe a video. What I will say for now is if you come here, try the tomatoes and olives in the markets. Fresh fruit for breakfast; peaches, nectarines, apples, bananas, are great for starting the day. Top it off with a cappuccino. It is a great way to start the day, especially if you are saving money. If you fancy splashing out, try the Cornettos. These are not the ice creams we are used to. Although they might make you want to sing the song from the advert, this is a croissant injected with pistachio cream or orange marmalade. Or, if you can find it, an apple and honey flavoured sauce—a particular favourite of mine.

If you fancy a dessert, you couldn't ask for more or much better.

Cannoli is a thick pastry dish, of supposed Arab origin, filled with thick ricotta cheese, sprinkled with various sweet treats; cherry, chocolate and pistachio. The men would go to war and, as a reward for surviving, they would be given a cannoli by their wives upon return (fair deal…) What surprised me was that the cannoli are meant to represent a penis. So not sure what to make of the men, surviving a war, surviving the journey back and nibbling on a tasty, cream-filled representation of a penis. Whatever the story, it's a damn good dessert. A favourite would be the pistachio flavoured version. Pistachio, a slightly salted and roasted nut, is an excellent flavour for the cream in the Cannoli or Cornetto and ice cream.

Ice cream is a favourite dessert in Sicily. Something to cool you down on those hot 30C days, or to complement an excellent main meal. The flavours and taste have been fantastic. A recommendation is to go to the marina. There is a small restaurant/cafe which has a whole host of different flavoured ice cream, which seem to have more cream, more natural flavour and less sugar, creating a perfect dessert to pass away the hours watching the ships roll in.

I have added a simple Italian pasta recipe that I cooked whilst out there. If you are looking for some ingredients, I would happily recommend the old market in Ortigia, on Vicolo Bagnara, which is next to the temple of Apollo. You can't miss this temple, as it is one of the first things you see as you come over the two bridges that connect the main island to Ortigia.

Ingredients:

1 kg ripe tomatoes

6 cloves of garlic

Olive oil

A handful of fresh pasta, which can be bought at the market.

Method:

I always find it is best to prep the ingredients first so that they can all go into the pan quickly.

First, roughly chop the tomatoes. Peel and finely slice 4 cloves of garlic and place them in a large frying pan with 3 tablespoons of olive oil. Place over a medium heat and cook until fragrant but not coloured. The garlic should be covered in a thin layer of oil and constantly moved to stop the colouring.

Then bring to a simmer and leave to cook for 45 minutes, or until reduced and delicious.

Peel and finely chop the remaining garlic, then fry in the sauce for 1 to 2 minutes.

Cook the pasta in a large pan of salted boiling water for 3 minutes, or until al dente. Spoon the pasta into the sauce, adding a good splash of cooking water to loosen and a drizzle of extra virgin olive oil.

Get your basil, and tear by hand and add to the sauce and cook for 1 minute.

Add the pasta and on a high heat cook the sauce and pasta together for one minute. Delicious served with a leafy salad dressed with good-quality balsamic vinegar and olive oil.

Chapter 7

Never Bring a Knife to a Mathematician Fight

***

Over the weeks I have been here, I've found it is truly amazing how much history is embedded into the rock and architecture of the city and its surrounding outskirts. No matter how deep you dig and delve, there is still more to find.

Each narrow street and passageway on the island of Ortigia can still hold something new that you've not seen or noticed before. Huge double doorways bar entry into courtyards that seem to open at random times of the day. If you step inside the courtyards, you generally find clean and crisp sandstone walls and volcanic rock floors.

The courtyards host music, residents, tourists, bars and cafes; each with their similar stone, yet an entirely different style of design such as Baroque, Greek, medieval, modern and Arabic.

Churches are scattered throughout the city, some now empty, some with art, such as Caravaggio, who for a time lived on the island and paid his way by selling his services and art to the church.

There are other hidden wonders to be found which includes the two museums dedicated to Archimedes. One is almost next to the Caravaggio church in Piazza Duomo. Once you have paid, you will be given a set of headphones, which react and tell a different story in each room you enter and on the object you are nearest. However, the first room you enter in the Archimedes' museum is huge and feels like a barn for its size. It takes you on a journey of Archimedes and the city by projecting images on all four walls, in a beautiful attempt to place you inside

Ancient Greek Ortigia. I've honestly never been in anything quite like it. Exceptional, especially as I've been to the major theme parks and museums in the U.K., some in Europe, and the US as well as Disneyland.

From the barn-sized room, you go into rooms demonstrating his inventions and mathematics. They try to demonstrate his mathematical principals with toys and games, and you think you've mastered some of his work and concepts. However, in the end, your bubble of intelligence is burst and you're told only a handful of people in the world can truly understand his work. Quite incredible considering the man existed 2000 years ago.

I guess that shows to some extent why Archimedes' war machines kicked Roman butt. They say never take a knife to a gunfight. I'm more concerned if they have a genius mathematician. His weapons were devastating, weapons including a 'death ray'. That last one is not a joke but maybe just a myth.

The stories, written over a hundred years later, describe various weapons the genius built for the defence of Syracuse. He rebuilt catapults and bolt throwers which could fire beyond normal distance for the time. If the Roman ships got past this, Archimedes had created some sort of hook that could attach itself to the Roman ship and, most likely using a counterweight, lift the ship onto its side and sink it. We also have accounts of a 'death ray', which was written about 150 years later, that was reported to be able to set ships on fire. In recent years, some TV shows and scientist have attempted to rebuild the 'death ray' with some varying success. Still, the city did fall to the Romans when a citizen of Syracuse opened the gates for them one night.

Archimedes was supposedly killed that night. Stories as to how he died do vary; the most famous being that he was sat at his desk and refused to move when Roman guards entered his property. His reason being that he was working on his calculations and did not want to be disturbed or moved just because the city was being ransacked. So, a Roman centurion struck him down.

Some other factors have been attributed to this mathematical genius. I will not delve into his mathematics too profoundly. From what I've understood, he calculated the size and depth of a cylinder and sphere, as well as realising they are the same in size. He also managed to calculate the weight of an object by placing it in water. A king had given him a complex puzzle, to see how much gold had been placed in the king's crown. One night, while getting into a bath, as the water went up, the solution jumped into his head. He could weigh the crown and an equal amount of gold into a bath, the density of a different metal would release a different amount of water. He was so excited that he jumped out, and ran down the street, shouting 'Eureka' meaning 'I found it.' An intelligent moment, arguably lacking wisdom as he was naked.

Finally, and there is some proof and reason to believe this was possibly constructed by Archimedes, there is the Antikythera mechanism. This is a mechanism that could predict the cycle of planets, the Sun, the Moon and the Earth, and was discovered off the coast of an island called Antikythera in 1902. Its creation can be attributed to some extent to Archimedes by the Roman general who took the city and brought two similarly described devices back to Rome. The device is so advanced that a British physicist once said it would be 'like finding a jet fighter in King Tut's tomb.' This is arguably one of the first computers in existence, yet it was built roughly 2000 years ago.

If you fancy another dive into a museum, there is the Da Vinci and Archimedes museum, less than a few hundred meters away. More Da Vinci than Archimedes. Again, containing all sorts of contraptions, most of which you can tug and pull, from Da Vinci's pulleys and levers to his hang-glider. Another genius of Italy, but to my knowledge no association to Ortigia other than enjoying and learning from the work of Archimedes. If you're into his work, I'd still recommend it. The museum, the island and the two geniuses can inspire you.

There are other places to visit as well: The Archaeological Park, which has life-size versions of their weapons. Da Vinci developed arguably the first tank. The park also contains a Roman amphitheatre, a Greek theatre and a sacrificial monument, all of which I will save for later as I'm hoping to see my first outdoor play there this week.

On a final note, on the first Sunday of every month, all the museums on the island are free. Considering there is all of this and a national museum next to the archaeological park, there is plenty of culture and history you can get stuck into on a Sunday.

Chapter 8

🎭 Plays, Performances & Politics 🎭

***

If you are looking for some culture and entertainment, you can't go far wrong with Syracuse's Greek amphitheatre. There are others on the island, some hidden in the most unlikely locations. I once found one hidden in a tall-looking bank, with a stream cutting in front of it, and tall reeds covering the stone steps. There is also the famous one based in Taormina, with its views of Mount Etna. You can see an image from the Taormina amphitheatre on my YouTube channel: Welcome World Walker.

Based on the mainland, it's set in the old bedrock, carved out by the Greeks who lived here two thousand years ago. The place has been regenerated from farmland into a modern outdoor theatre and with the weather being so good, the plays are hardly ever interrupted by the weather gods. They operate for three months of the year, May to June, and show two different plays each month.

The theatre dates back to the 5th-century B.C. and was at least operational for 900 years. Records of it then renewed in the 1500s when Spanish King Charles V destroyed the scenery stonework and upper parts of the theatre to build fortifications on the island of Ortigia. Finally, in the early 1900s, Sicilians began to restore and reuse the theatre for plays. Today it is heavily modernised and yet endeavours to keep as much of the traditional parts of the theatre as possible. Wood replaces the rock. Cushions are available. Electric lights and sound systems support the late-night performances and it even has an instant translation system, which gives you the play in English.

If you go on a relatively quiet night, there is even space to lie down, listening to the play, while staring at the stars and the rising moon.

When you arrive, you walk past other Ancient Greek monuments and are greeted by officers in military-esque uniform, standing with sabres or sitting on horses. The sun shines down on the white stone, creating a stunning white glow that lights up everywhere and everything.

As you go up the steps to find your seats, you begin to see that the Greeks really did pick fantastic locations for their theatres. Not only had they found a rock to carve into that could make a U-shaped theatre but it also gave stunning views of the bay in Ortigia, which you can still see today on the highest seats. The closer, the more expensive. I decided to take my friend Marthe with me. The seats we had were €30 and you could sit wherever you liked in the section. You can buy the tickets at the theatre, and it does help to have a little Italian. There are some key Italian phrases at the back of this book. If you are bringing kids they can come in for free, but make sure you bring I.D. regardless of their age.

As the night draws in and lights go on, you can hear a

stream babbling behind the upper seats. The stream is connected to an Ancient Greek aqueduct, which is still in operation today. It draws water from a hill several miles away and runs past the theatre, supposedly designed to allow the theatre to be flooded if required.

The play we saw was Aristophanes' *The Knights* (almost 2500 years old), which is a political comedy, a commentary on Athens, and the city's fight against the Spartans. It discusses both the foolishness of the upper and lower classes of Athens, with a modern interpretation that clearly criticised current Italian politicians as well as the people. It tells of a sausage maker who attempts to rise to political leadership through selling lies and foolish ideas. This seems more akin to a Donald Trump leadership, except the guy had big hands and a lot of long sausages, so clearly it must have been resembling some other political leader. For a night of outdoor entertainment, you could not ask for more and I would thoroughly recommend attending this venue; the humour was timeless and the setting romantic.

What more could you ask for on a Thursday night?

You can buy bus tickets online using the link below:
http://www.indafondazione.org/it/

You can also buy tickets for the amphitheatre productions:
http://www.indafondazione.org/it/stagione-2018/

Chapter 9

 Volcano

***

One of the most spectacular sites of Sicily is Mount Etna also known as Mama Etna, a beautiful mountain. It was also one of the most significant reasons for me coming to the island.

She can be seen from a huge chunk of the island, and she is deceptively big.

It was the clashing of the European and African tectonic plates that have created her. She is still classed as active and roughly 3,329 meters in height.

Her history in written records goes back to 300 B.C. Although the creation of the island and volcano goes back to 500,000 B.C. 35,000 years ago, the volcano erupted and sent ash as far as Rome. The Greeks mention her, as do the Romans. The Titan Typhoon defeated by the Greek gods was placed underneath and trapped forever, with the blacksmith, Vulcan, residing and working inside the mountain. In 400/300 B.C. the volcano erupted, stopping armies advancing on the city of Syracuse.

The next eruption was in 120 B.C, which caused so much damage that the Roman government gave the city a tax exemption for ten years. Records, unfortunately, become sparse and we don't hear much until 1669 when Mama Etna destroyed ten villages and reached the city walls of Catania. The number of deaths varies from under 100 to 15,000. Records vary and depend on the event. 24 years later, a major earthquake took place and destroyed a large chunk of the same eastern area of the island.

In the more modern period, I've read of at least ten major eruptions taking place, one so large that the ash was landing in Libya and visible from space. Knowing all this, I still choose to live here along with the rest of the population and all the tourists that come here.

It's exciting in some ways to have such a magnificent piece of geography ready to erupt at any point on your doorstep. It can give you an extra sense of being alive as well as keeping you on your toes. I'm sure there is a Trump comparison there somewhere. Unlike Trump, I assume everyone wishes the volcano was able to tweet when it was going to blow up!

I've taken more precautions here than with any of the terrorist threats in London, packing a waterproof bag with the equipment mentioned in a previous chapter.

I decided with my friend Marthe to visit Mama. It's surprisingly easy to get to from Syracuse. The train gets you to the city of Catania for €6.50 single and a bus to the midpoint of the volcano was €6. To buy your ticket you walk from the train station across the roundabout, which has the world's longest zebra crossing, past all the buses to the other side. You are looking for a street called 'Via don Luigi Sturzo'. The street contains the AST bus ticket office.

You can find a friendly, big and burly ex-Italian international rugby player in there, who's very friendly and helpful.

You take the bus from the bus stop inside the roundabout and make your way to the volcano in comfort, with air conditioning and a relaxed atmosphere. I was not sure whether to be reassured or not with the relaxed drivers. Our first driver was a great comfort, his knees up against the dashboard on the phone to friends and family, hands-free of course. We stopped in a small village part-way at noon, and our relaxing journey continued. As we got off the bus, the sound of gunfire exploded all around, leaving us unsure if it was terrorists or the volcano. It was neither; it was the locals casually setting off booming fireworks to let everyone know it was midday!

The final stage of the bus journey was interesting. The Italian driver and his friend sat on the other front seat, showing their eternal comfort driving up one of the most active volcanos in the world, decided to switch seats while the bus was moving.

The whole of that experience made me question a lot how much I should care about driving up Mama. Should I be worried by these drivers or reassured that they feel so comfortable to act this way with an active volcano underneath them and us?

We continued up winding roads but nothing steep, like on other mountain adventures I have been on. More and more of the black solid rock streams could be seen, mostly solid and some porous. They snaked and steered through the green grass. We finally arrived at the southern section summit and could see the next part was more climbing.

Beautiful scenic views stretched out before us, with clouds dancing in front of us as well as hanging over the beaches miles down below and into the distance. The next stage was to take the cable car up to the next point, which was €30. I did find quad bikes that would have been €50 each for 1 hour, with a guide. Something I might do in the future. I will also point out that if you have the boots, you could walk to the top of the volcano and there were plenty of people doing so. If you are intending to do this, make sure you take the right equipment and I would always recommend hiring a guide. The mountain is so vast and the terrain so similar in appearance that it could be easy to get lost.

We took suntan lotion, changeable clothes and bottles of water. As for clothing, though it was 30C down the bottom of the mountain, as we climbed the temperature dropped so shorts and T-shirt soon turned into a hoody, scarf and waterproof jacket as we climbed each section. I would recommend not wearing white shorts as it is a little sooty up there.

The cable car took us to the next section, giving us an even better and clearer view of the peaks, where smoke was billowing out of cracks and the gigantic cones. Once at this second stage, the mountain had a Martian feel to the landscape. Red rocks scattered the landscape, with black, cooled lava streams shredding through the red landscape following gravity to the bottom of the mountain. We then discovered that there was another section to climb and that was to be reached via large, all-terrain,

Mercedes anti-volcano buses: Huge, grey, metal-reinforced vehicles with tyres almost 6ft in height. It was another €32 to get on board and be given a guide.

This is where it becomes interesting, as the guided tours I had discovered online had varied in cost and I had found prices for €38 – €80.

I was beginning to think that the guided tours you pay for online would have been worth it and money saving. Taormina seemed like the cheapest location to go from to get to the mountain.

We paid and the bus trundled its way through ash-covered roads with the bus driver stopping to show ash-covered snow still sitting on the mountainside. We came to a stop in a small parking area with a couple of wooden cabins. We were ushered out and into groups. A middle-aged man then showed us the way to the most recent volcanic activity.

The huge volcano vents were in the shape of giant cones

and some were the length and width of several football pitches and went to a depth of a 7/8 storey building. There was one vent, that the guide claimed 50 million tons of lava had spewed from only a few years ago, and that just next to it was a river of now solid lava that scaled around the side of this cone. The whole experience was one of awe and wonder with a healthy dose of fear that it could go off again at any moment. We walked around the edge of the cone's upper lip and once fully around we began our descent. We took the truck to the cable car then cable car to the southern point, where some well-deserved grub could be procured. Overall, it was a most excellent journey that felt scary, awe-inspiring and thrilling with a real sense of 'anything can happen'. I can't compare this to anything I've tried before to get a similar set of emotions.

The best part was the realisation that from December until April this area turns into a ski and snowboard park, with the added excitement of knowing you could be boarding along the mountain, seeing geysers and volcanic smoke drift past you at any moment. I intend to go again regularly from December to April.

For train tickets you can purchase them from Trainline Europe | European Train TravelAd the link is below:

www.trainline.eu

For guided tours of Mount Etna I have added the link below:

https://m.viator.com/Sicily-attractions/Mount-Etna/d205-a7649?seotype=attraction

Chapter 10

A Train Ride to Remember

***

For €42 and booked in a month in advance, you can take a train ride from Syracuse, stop in Naples to change and then first-class the rest of the way to Rome.

Included in this journey I saw a train being eaten by a boat, two volcanos, the Amalfi coast and an array of interesting characters from all over the globe, including people having sex. Pictures not included.

With my plans being ad hoc and my time ending in Syracuse, mainly due to ongoing contract and instability at work, I decided to head back home and was able to tick another thing off my bucket list.

I've always wanted to do the Orient Express but, to be honest, what I've always wanted to do is get a horse and a dog and make my way across Europe. Maybe in another lifetime.

The station in Syracuse, to my knowledge, is a creation left over from Mussolini's era. A story for another day. One thing you can say is how beautiful the station is with its huge ceilings, Roman pillars and marble floors, with a cool breeze running through it. The ticket machines are easy to use, with four languages available. Just make sure once you've bought the ticket you then find the little green and white devices on the platform or main room and get your ticket stamped. €50 fine if you don't!

The train was excellent; spacious and with good air conditioning. Something I will be writing more about was an easy conversation started up with three Australians. All were taking time off from work, with two of them travelling across Europe. The other was living in Berlin. Striking up a conversation was easy; I simply asked where they were from, where they were headed and their thoughts of Syracuse. They have been featured below!

I've always thought, 'ask, listen and make the conversation fun when you can'.

I always said that to my football and basketball players and students.

'How many mouths do you have? How many ears do you have? Good, then listen twice as much as you talk, you'll grow quicker.'

~Alex Kerr

Just a simple life principle. The train pulled out of the station; we chatted, laughed, exchanged stories and took plenty of photos. The train from here to Rome was probably 75% sea views and then the rest valleys, hills, mountains and volcanos. I only wish I brought some food and not just water. So, I had to spend potentially 8 hours without any food! #Hangry.

The train passed Mount Etna one more time. I think I finally got how big a bastard it was and that there must have been one hell of an explosion on it at some point. The crater looked like it could have fitted a city inside of it. My attention returned to the coastline and the very confident couple casually playing on the beach. The girl was riding both waves and a man with no bikini bottom on. Her confidence was unparalleled as she smiled and waved at us in the passing train. The joke was on her, as I waved back. I'm sure she didn't see me, or the woman and her dog heading towards them…

The train stopped at several towns, Taormina and Messina. Taormina is worth a visit, with beautiful views of Mount Etna, mainland Italy and the sea in between. Definitely something I would like to discuss in a future book.

The coolest part had to be seeing the train pull into the port and being eaten by the boat. Carriages were placed in three rows, then, carried across the sea, fresh salty sea air on the deck and awesome ariancas, like a scotch egg, but instead of egg filed with rice and ragu (bolognese sauce).

The train soon continued, and we headed onto the Amalfi

Coast and Naples. Sun hit the sea and pierced through the ocean to reveal the ocean floor, while also shining onto the hills and mountains.

After 6 hours of travelling, we pulled into Naples to see another volcano looming in the distance. The size of this monster was just unbelievable, as well as the crater that had exploded a thousand years ago covering the town below in ash and lava.

The final stage was onto Rome—first class! I'd never done it before but for €3 extra, it was totally worth it: Huge leather seats, salty snacks and a damn tasty glass of prosecco. It pretty much paid for itself and a conversation was started again with an American couple who were friendly, chatty and amazed by this country, pretty much confirming my thoughts of the food, culture and lifestyle. We blitzed into Rome in an hour.

8 hours in total and was a pretty interesting way to replace the Orient Express.

Chapter 11

Final

***

This journey has been a fantastic one and I hope it either inspires you to travel, move and/or think of your own adventures. There were so many things to talk about, such as the tunnels under the main Piazza, or the castle at the far end of Ortigia, the cathedral on crypt on the mainland, the passion of the local supports for their local football team, the market near the marina, walking along the marina with a gelato as the sun sets, or the simple pleasures of the restaurants (there is a restaurant near the lagoon that has an indoor section with a glass floor, showing an ancient Greek bath that still has water running through it) and pizzerias. There are some great ones on Via del Crocifisso; one on the corner and one further down, which is hidden amongst the plants.

For a good coffee experience, the Duomo first thing in the morning is a stunning experience to sit, read, drink, talk and see the sunshine bounce off the marble flooring. However, make sure if you stay in this lovely city you go grab a coffee in as many of the areas as possible as well as explore the city on your own.

If you are keen, there are some videos on my YouTube channel: Welcome World Walker, and on my blog on WordPress: Welcome World Walker, showing lots of pictures and videos depicting Sicily.

Some Helpful Italian Phrases:

A tip for greeting Italians: When you meet someone for the first time it is common to shake hands. When you get to know and become more comfortable with each other, you can kiss each other on the cheek, which starts with the left cheek first.

Buongiorno! (bwohn-johr-noh)	Good morning!
Arrivederci! (ahr-ree-veh-dehr-chee)	Goodbye!
Ciao	Hello! and Good-bye!
Come ti chiama? (koh-meh see kyah-mah)	What is your name?
Mi chiamo... (mee kyah-moh)	My name is. . .
Come stai? (koh-meh stahy)	How are you?
Bene (beh-neh)	Good/fine
Si	Yes
No	No

Being Polite

Grazie (grah-tsee-eh)	Thank You
Per favore (pehr fah-voh-reh)	Please
Mi dispiace (mee dees-pyah-cheh)	I'm sorry

Italian Numbers

1	Uno
2	Due
3	Tre
4	Quattro
5	Cinque
6	Sei
7	Sette
8	Otto
9	Nove
10	Dieci

Directions

Sinistra Sih-nih-strah	Left
Destra Dehstrah	Right
Sempre dritto Sehmpreh drihtoh	Straight ahead

A Summary of Websites to Check Out and Help with your Journey:

Travel Insurance:

https://www.moneysavingexpert.com/travel-insurance/

Flights:

https://www.skyscanner.net

Trains:

https://www.thetrainline.com/trains/europe

Banking and Spending:

https://www.metrobankonline.co.uk/

Mobile phones and internet:

www.three.co.uk

Many thanks to all those who have supported me:

Gran, Dad, Jason & Laura.

Marthe Mostervik x

Natalie Kirk

Julia-Carolin Zeng

Charity & Laure for letting me use your house to write!

Agata Leocata

Except as provided by the Copyright Act 1956, The Copyright, Designs and Patents Act 1988, Copyright and Related Rights Regulations 2003, no part of this publication may be reproduced, stored in a retrieval system or transmitted in any form or by any means without the prior written permission of the publisher.

Printed in Great Britain
by Amazon